2

MEGAWORDS

Multisyllabic Words for
Reading, Spelling, and Vocabulary

POLLY BAYRD · KRISTIN JOHNSON

EDUCATORS PUBLISHING SERVICE
Cambridge and Toronto

Design by Persis Barron Levy

Typesetting by Rebecca Royen

Educators Publishing Service
800.225.5750
www.epsbooks.com

Printed in the U.S.A.
ISBN 0-8388-1828-5
978-0-8388-1828-2
6 7 8 9 PPG 10 09 08

CONTENTS

TO THE STUDENT

Megawords 2: Multisyllabic Words for Reading, Spelling, and Vocabulary is the second in a series of books designed to help you read and spell words that contain two or more syllables. The words are organized into lists according to their phonetic structure. Worksheets following each list explain and help you practice the rules or patterns found in that particular group of words. Some exercises focus on reading the words; others focus on spelling or vocabulary.

Megawords is designed to meet your individual learning needs. You and your teacher can decide which lists you need to study (and which you already know) by interpreting your results on the Check Test. You may need to focus on reading *and* spelling. Or you may need to use **Megawords** only to improve spelling skills. You and your teacher can record your progress on the Accuracy Checklist at the back of your book.

We think that it is important for you to be able to 1) sound out words and 2) learn to read them proficiently and fluently. You and your teacher will set a reading rate goal. When you can read the words easily and automatically, you will be less likely to forget the words and you can concentrate on reading for meaning instead of on sounding out words. You can keep track of your reading rate on the Proficiency Graph at the end of your book.

Megawords 2 focuses on common prefixes and suffixes found in two-syllable words. It teaches you the spelling rules for adding suffixes and the meanings of prefixes and some Latin roots. **Megawords 2** assumes that you have mastered the syllabic concepts presented in **Megawords 1.**

We hope that you will be interested in checking out your skills in reading and spelling multisyllabic words—in seeing what you know and what you need to learn. In addition, we hope that you will enjoy tackling new word groups and mastering them. We think that multisyllabic words, when presented clearly and in patterned groups, can be challenging and fun. We sincerely hope that you enjoy and experience success with **Megawords.**

Polly Bayrd
Kristin Johnson

LIST 9: CONSONANT SUFFIXES AND PLURALS*

-ly	-ful, -fully	-ment	-less	Plural -s	Plural -es
badly	careful	apartment	blameless	airplanes	ashes
completely	carefully	basement	careless	baskets	babies
finally	cheerful	government	childless	blankets	benches
friendly	cheerfully	movement	endless	blossoms	bodies
gladly	colorful	pavement	fearless	bubbles	boxes
hardly	faithful	payment	harmless	buttons	branches
lately	faithfully	placement	helpless	cabins	brushes
likely	fearful	shipment	homeless	camels	bushes
lonely	fearfully	statement	lifeless	candles	butterflies
lovely	forceful		pointless	farmers	churches
monthly	forcefully		priceless	fingers	cities
mostly	graceful	**–ness**	restless	gardens	classes
namely	gracefully	brightness	speechless	insects	copies
nearly	grateful	darkness	useless	manners	dishes
nicely	gratefully	goodness	worthless	monkeys	dresses
quickly	hateful	happiness		needles	glasses
quietly	helpful	illness		newspapers	inches
really	hopeful	kindness		notebooks	parties
safely	hopefully	likeness		persons	peaches
slowly	joyful	sadness		pickles	ponies
surely	painful	shyness		problems	puppies
swiftly	painfully	sickness		rabbits	sandwiches
widely	playful	soreness		squirrels	stories
yearly	playfully	stillness		subjects	studies
	skillful	weakness		tables	taxes
	thankful			turkeys	wishes
–ty	thankfully	**–some**		uncles	witches
ninety	truthful	bothersome		valleys	
safety	truthfully	handsome			
seventy	useful	lonesome			
sixty	wasteful	troublesome			
	wonderful	wholesome			

*All words on this list are practical spelling words. The teacher and student should decide together how many of these words the student will be responsible for spelling.

1

⭐ A suffix is a word part that comes at the end of a word. Sometimes it changes the meaning of a word (care-*ful*, care*less*) and sometimes it changes the way the word is used in a sentence, i.e., its part of speech (dress-*ing*, dress*ed*, dress*y*).

A root is the main word part to which suffixes are attached (*slow*ly, un*sink*able).

A consonant suffix is a suffix that begins with a consonant. Learn to recognize these consonant suffixes: *-ly, -ty, -ful, -fully, -ment, -some, -less,* and *-ness.*

Do not change the root when adding a consonant suffix.

➡ Circle the suffixes in the following words.

skillful	pointless	government	sickness
nicely	lonesome	faithfully	handsome
movement	safely	blameless	ninety
truthfully	soreness	graceful	widely

➡ Match each root with a suffix to make a real word. Then say the word as you write it.

safe
   ty   *safety*
   ment
   less

shy
   ty
   ness
   ment

color
   ness
   ful
   ly
   some

fear
   ly
   ment
   fully
   ful

use
   ty
   less
   some

thank
   ly
   ness
   ful

whole
   ness
   fully

base
   ment
   ty

➤ Your teacher will dictate some words. Repeat each word, isolate the root, and spell it. Then write the whole word, saying it aloud as you spell.

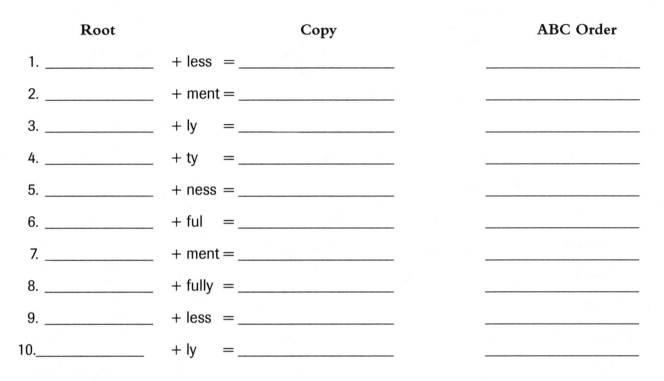

	Root	Copy	ABC Order
1.	_____ + less =	_____	_____
2.	_____ + ment =	_____	_____
3.	_____ + ly =	_____	_____
4.	_____ + ty =	_____	_____
5.	_____ + ness =	_____	_____
6.	_____ + ful =	_____	_____
7.	_____ + ment =	_____	_____
8.	_____ + fully =	_____	_____
9.	_____ + less =	_____	_____
10.	_____ + ly =	_____	_____

➤ Your teacher will dictate some more words. Repeat each word, isolate the suffix, and spell it. Then write the whole word, saying it aloud as you spell.

		Suffix	Copy	ABC Order
11.	kind +	_____	= _____	_____
12.	hope +	_____	= _____	_____
13.	friend +	_____	= _____	_____
14.	care +	_____	= _____	_____
15.	ship +	_____	= _____	_____
16.	safe +	_____	= _____	_____
17.	end +	_____	= _____	_____
18.	lone +	_____	= _____	_____
19.	help +	_____	= _____	_____

➤ Now go back and write the words in each section in alphabetical order.

➤ In the following words, draw a line between the root and the suffix. Then pronounce each word as you write the root and suffix on the first two lines and the whole word on the third line.

	Root	Suffix	Word
lone|some	lone	some	lonesome
swiftly			
carefully			
pavement			
really			
priceless			
completely			
soreness			
basement			
finally			
wonderful			

➤ Unscramble the words and spell them correctly in the blanks. They all contain suffixes. The meanings and first letters are your clues to arranging the letters in the correct order.

1. ahluftnk   t_____   full of thanks

2. ywsoll   s_____   not quickly

3. seldesn   e_____   never ending

4. slestnlis   st_____   total quiet

5. eiynnt   n_____   comes after 89

6. cepshessel   s_____   unable to speak

Review

A _____ is a word part that comes at the end of a word.

A _____ suffix is a suffix that begins with a consonant.

A _____ is the main word part to which suffixes are attached.

4

★ Most of the time, add *s* to a word to make it plural. But if a word ends in *s, sh, ch, z,* or *x,* add *es* to make it plural.

➡ Add *es* or *s* to the following words to make them plural. Say the words to yourself as you spell them. Notice that adding *es* adds another syllable to the word, but adding *s* does not change the number of syllables.

box _es_   _boxes_   uncle_____   _____

camel_____   _____   church_____   _____

inch_____   _____   dress_____   _____

farmer_____   _____   brush_____   _____

peach_____   _____   table_____   _____

class_____   _____   squirrel_____   _____

manner_____   _____   wish_____   _____

tax_____   _____   sandwich_____   _____

bench_____   _____   blanket_____   _____

bubble_____   _____   dish_____   _____

witch_____   _____   glass_____   _____

➡ Find and circle all of the words above in the puzzle below. The words can be found in a straight line across or up and down.

```
B R U S H E S G L A S B D S A N D W I  C H E S
O B N H T A B L E S O L I Q U D R I  M H M B T
X O C C L A T A X E S A S U N I E T A U A U I
S P E A C H E S C L I N H E C S S C N R N B N
A L L M C L A S S E S K E R L H S H N C N B C
B O X E S O B E N C H E S A E S E E E H E L H
B U B L E W I S H E S T A X S N S S T E R E E
C L A S E F A R M E R S Q U I R R E L S S S S
```

★ If a word ends in a *y* with a consonant just before it, change the *y* to *i* and add *es* to make the word plural (*city ⟶ cities*).

If a word ends in *y* with a vowel before it, add *s* (*valley ⟶ valleys; boy ⟶ boys; play ⟶ plays*).

➡ Circle the letter just before the *y*. Then spell the plurals of these words.

	Plural	**ABC order**
study	_____	_____
turkey	_____	_____
party	_____	_____
baby	_____	_____
copy	_____	_____
pony	_____	_____
story	_____	_____
valley	_____	_____
lady	_____	_____
body	_____	_____
puppy	_____	_____
monkey	_____	_____
butterfly	_____	_____

➡ Now go back and write the words in alphabetical order.

Review

To make a word that ends in vowel-*y* plural, _____

To make a word that ends in consonant-*y* plural, _____
_____

➡ Your teacher will dictate words that have suffixes. Spell them under the correct heading.

-ly	*-ful*	*-fully*
_____	_____	_____
_____	_____	_____
_____	_____	_____

-ment	*-less*	*-ness*
_____	_____	_____
_____	_____	_____

-ty	*-some*
_____	_____

➡ Your teacher will dictate plural words. Decide which rule to apply and spell the words under the correct headings.

Add *s*	Add *es*	Change *y* to *i* and add *es*
_____	_____	_____
_____	_____	_____
_____	_____	_____

Proofing Practice

Two common words are misspelled in each of the sentences below. Correct them as shown.

1. When the train ~~finaly~~ *finally* arrived, it was ninty minutes late.

2. We were very greatful for the hansome gift.

3. It is hard to be chearful when you lose a puppie.

4. New York has more newspaipers than most sites.

5. Mr. Delgado asked the playfull children to talk more queitly.

★ The suffix *-ful* changes the root from a noun (naming word) to an adjective (describing word). The suffix *-fully* changes the root to an adverb (a word that describes action).

➡ Read the sentences and write the word with the correct suffix in each blank.

1. grace   Coretta dances_____. She is a
   _____person.
   (adverb) / (adjective)

2. care   Be_____! You must wash the china very
   _____.
   (adjective) / (adverb)

3. thank   Sandy was_____for all the gifts.
   (adjective)

4. hope   "Things will work out for the best," she said_____.
   (adverb)

5. pain   Carlos_____moved his right leg.
   (adverb)

6. help   Children should learn how to be_____around the house.
   (adjective)

7. color   The leaves are_____this time of year.
   (adjective)

8. cheer   Shawn always works_____.
   (adverb)

9. skill   Linda is_____at her job.
   (adjective)

10. hate   Milton was so mad that he was_____toward everyone.
    (adjective)

11. play   The kitten_____chased the ball of string.
    (adverb)

12. fear   Terry_____peeked into the dark basement.
    (adverb)

13. faith   Odysseus'_____wife waited for him for over twenty years.
    (adjective)

14. waste   It is_____to throw away aluminum cans when we can
    recycle them.
    (adjective)

Review

A_____is a naming word. An_____is a describing word. An_____describes action.

★ Adding the suffix -*ness* to a root that is an adjective (describing word) changes it to a noun (naming word).

➡ Add the suffix -*ness* to each root. Then write the noun in the right sentence.

good__ __ __ __   sad__ __ __ __   sick__ __ __ __   still__ __ __ __

bright__ __ __ __   dark__ __ __ __   weak__ __ __ __

1. The_____of the floodlights blinded her for a minute.

2. Francis was upset by the death of his pet. You could see the_____in his face.

3. Jan missed school last week because of_____.

4. The_____of the night and the howl of a lone wolf frightened us.

5. My grandma is so funny. She always says, "My_____, won't we have a lark!"

6. Because of a_____in his back, Mr. Palmer cannot lift anything heavy.

7. In the middle of the hurricane there was a period of eerie_____.

★ Adding the suffix -*less* to a root that is a noun (naming word) changes it to an adjective (describing word).

➡ Add the suffix -*less* to each root. Then write the adjective in the right sentence.

worth__ __ __ __   use__ __ __ __   rest__ __ __ __

life__ __ __ __   fear__ __ __ __   care__ __ __ __

8. Megan did not sleep well. She spent a_____night.

9. Yesterday Donald was arrested because he wrote ten_____checks.

10. The party was no fun at all. It was completely _____.

11. I have no idea what to do with this gift. The Bartons always give

_____gifts.

12. The _____children went rock climbing every weekend.

13. Tracy missed number seven on the grammar quiz. She made a

_____mistake.

➡ Fill in each blank with one of these suffixes so that the sentence makes sense.

-some   -ly   -ty   -ment

1. I will glad_____ help you if I can.

2. Marvin is very good-looking. I think he is quite hand_____.

3. Have you made your last pay_____ on the loan?

4. There should be no move_____ when I try to take your picture.

5. It isn't like_____ that you could read that entire book in one evening.

6. I don't like to be by myself all weekend. I get lone_____ for company.

7. When there is snow on the pave_____, the children rollerskate in the base_____.

8. Donna is still looking for a job. She would like to work for the state govern_____.

9. After nine_____ days on the job, I am final_____ getting the hang of it.

10. We had to move from our apart_____ when the landlord raised our rent by

    seven_____ dollars.

11. Mr. Gibbons ate only whole_____ foods: nuts, berries, fruit, and grains.

12. Ms. Wisty makes a month_____ payment on her car.

13. The fearless raccoons were very bother_____ when they raided our food pack at night.

➡ Copy the words that have suffixes under the correct headings.

-some	-ly	-ty	-ment
_____	_____	_____	_____
_____	_____	_____	_____
_____	_____		_____
_____	_____		_____
			_____
			_____

➡ Read the following sentences and circle all the words from List 9 that you can find.

1. Three squirrels ran playfully around the bushes.

2. Babies are completely helpless.

3. Newspapers in large cities are widely read by many persons.

4. Although Alan seemed cheerful and friendly, he really was lonesome for his family.

5. Lately the children have been careless about their manners.

6. Martha is careful to keep the playful puppies in the basement.

7. Churches do not have to pay taxes to the government.

8. In the stillness of the night, Agnes quietly read two short stories.

9. The blossoms on the branches are lovely this spring.

10. It is useless and wasteful to make so many copies of that statement.

11. The graceful dancers waited hopefully for the results of the tryout.

➡ Take out a piece of blank paper. Your teacher will dictate three of the sentences above for you to write.

➡ Now select ten words from List 9 and create a short story or a descriptive paragraph that uses those words. Be creative and avoid repetition!

Reading Accuracy: Demonstrate your accuracy in reading and spelling List 9 words. Your teacher will select ten words to read and ten practical spelling words for you to spell. Record your scores on the Accuracy Checklist. Work toward 90–100 percent accuracy.

Reading Proficiency: Now build up your reading fluency with List 9 words. Decide on your rate goal with your teacher. Record your progress on the Proficiency Graph.

My goal for reading List 9 is _____ words per minute with two or fewer errors.

LIST 10: VOWEL SUFFIXES AND SPELLING RULES*

-ing	-er, -est	-en	-y	Mixed Suffixes Drop-the-e Rule	Mixed Suffixes Doubling and Y Rule
adding	brighter	beaten	cloudy	biting	biggest
asking	brightest	brighten	curly	blamed	bitten
banking	cleaner	dampen	dirty	broken	clipper
barking	cleanest	eaten	eighty	caring	digging
bringing	colder	fallen	healthy	chosen	drummer
buying	coldest	frighten	lucky	dancing	earlier
crying	darker	golden	messy	driven	earliest
dressing	deepest	harden	mighty	frozen	easier
drying	faster	lengthen	rainy	frozen	floppy
falling	fastest	sharpen	risky	icy	funniest
farming	fewer	shorten	rusty	largest	funny
fishing	greater	wooden	sandy	latest	gotten
helping	greatest	woolen	sleepy	leaving	hidden
jumping	higher		snowy	loving	hotter
milking	highest	**-ish**	sticky	placing	lazier
packing	longer		stormy	riding	madder
planting	longest	British	tricky	safest	muddy
playing	lowest	foolish	wealthy	shining	prettiest
printing	nearer	selfish	windy	skating	quitting
raining	nearest	Spanish		sliding	robber
singing	older			smiling	rotten
standing	oldest			smoky	saddest
starting	smaller			stylish	shopping
studying	sooner			taken	sunny
swinging	strongest			tasty	swimming
thinking	warmer			using	wedding
walking	younger			wider	whipping
wanting	youngest			writing	

*All words on this list are practical spelling words. The teacher and student should decide together how many of these words the student will be responsible for spelling.

★ A **vowel suffix** is a suffix that begins with a vowel. Learn to recognize these vowel suffixes: *-ing, -er, -est, -ish, -y,* and *-en.*

➡ Circle the suffixes in the following words. Be careful; what looks like a suffix may really be part of a root. You should have a complete word left over if you have circled the suffix.

lifting	soften	wren	selfish
spring	nearer	sleepy	squish
lowest	guest	darker	ringing
dirty	studying	prefer	swing

➡ Match each root with a suffix to make a real word. Then say the word as you write it.

	en		est		ish
think	y	slow	en	fool	est
	ing		y		en

_____   _____   _____

	en		est		er
sing	est	beat	en	gold	en
	ing		y		ing

_____   _____   _____

➡ Make two words out of the roots and suffixes below.

	ing		en		y
talk	est	length	est	clean	er
	er		y		est

_____   _____   _____

_____   _____   _____

★ A **consonant suffix** is a suffix that begins with a consonant. *-ly, -ty, -ful, -fully, -ment, -some, -less,* and *-ness* are consonant suffixes.

A **vowel suffix** is a suffix that begins with a vowel. The vowel suffixes in List 10 are *-ing, -er, -est, -ish, -y,* and *-en.*

➡ Circle at least twelve suffixes in the phrases and sentences below.

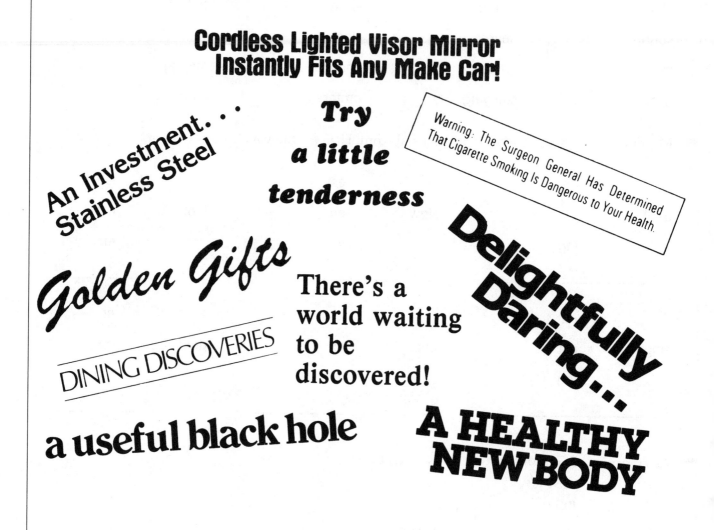

Cordless Lighted Visor Mirror Instantly Fits Any Make Car!

An Investment. . . Stainless Steel

Try a little tenderness

Warning: The Surgeon General Has Determined That Cigarette Smoking Is Dangerous to Your Health.

Golden Gifts

DINING DISCOVERIES

There's a world waiting to be discovered!

Delightfully Daring...

a useful black hole

A HEALTHY NEW BODY

➡ List three consonant suffixes and three vowel suffixes that you circled.

Consonant Suffixes	Vowel Suffixes
_____	_____
_____	_____
_____	_____

Your teacher will dictate some words. Repeat each word, isolate the root, and spell it. Then write the whole word, saying it aloud as you spell.

	Root		Copy	ABC Order
1.	_____	+ ish =	_____	_____
2.	_____	+ er =	_____	_____
3.	_____	+ ing =	_____	_____
4.	_____	+ y =	_____	_____
5.	_____	+ en =	_____	_____
6.	_____	+ est =	_____	_____
7.	_____	+ ing =	_____	_____
8.	_____	+ y =	_____	_____
9.	_____	+ en =	_____	_____
10.	_____	+ er =	_____	_____

Isolate, pronounce, and spell the suffix you hear in the words your teacher dictates. Then write the whole word saying it aloud as you spell.

	Suffix		Copy	ABC Order
11.	hard +	_____ =	_____	_____
12.	bright +	_____ =	_____	_____
13.	fool +	_____ =	_____	_____
14.	want +	_____ =	_____	_____
15.	near +	_____ =	_____	_____
16.	bark +	_____ =	_____	_____
17.	gold +	_____ =	_____	_____
18.	health +	_____ =	_____	_____
19.	old +	_____ =	_____	_____

Now go back and write the words in each section in alphabetical order.

➡ Divide the following words between the root and the suffix. Then pronounce each word as you write the root and suffix on the first two lines and the whole word on the third line.

	Root	**Suffix**	**Word**
longer	_____	_____	_____
fastest	_____	_____	_____
sharpen	_____	_____	_____
tricky	_____	_____	_____
selfish	_____	_____	_____
dressing	_____	_____	_____
risky	_____	_____	_____
greatest	_____	_____	_____
singing	_____	_____	_____
frighten	_____	_____	_____
younger	_____	_____	_____

➡ Unscramble the words below and spell them correctly in the blanks. They all contain suffixes. The meaning and first letters are your clues to arranging the letters in the correct order.

1. hislofo   f_____   like a fool

2. dangdi   a_____   putting numbers together

3. yhtlaew   w_____   having much money

4. galwikn   w_____   slower than running

5. odenow   w_____   made of wood

6. tealcens   c_____   the most clean

Review

A consonant suffix begins with a _____.

A vowel suffix begins with a _____.

RULE

The **Doubling Rule**: If a root has one syllable, ends in one consonant, and has one vowel, double the consonant before adding a vowel suffix.

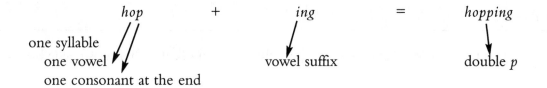

| | | *hop* | + | *ing* | = | *hopping* |

one syllable
one vowel
one consonant at the end

vowel suffix

double *p*

➡ Look at each root below and check for each condition of the Doubling Rule. If you have four checks, then double the final consonant before adding the suffix. If you have fewer than four checks, add the suffix without changing the root.

	one syllable	one vowel	ends in one consonant	adding a vowel suffix	Root + Suffix
1. sad + est	✔	✔	✔	✔	_saddest_
2. mud + y					_____
3. fright + en					_____
4. cold + er					_____
5. swim + ing					_____
6. like + ness					_____
7. rust + y					_____
8. bad + ly					_____
9. bit + en					_____
10. whip + ing					_____
11. skill + ful					_____
12. risk + y					_____
13. cold + est					_____
14. wood + en					_____

Review

The Doubling Rule: If a root has _____ syllable, ends in one _____, and has _____ vowel sound, double the final _____ before adding a _____ suffix *(hop + ing = hopping).*

➡ Add suffixes to the roots. Remember to apply the Doubling Rule when it is needed.

drum + er _____	clip + er _____
*farm + ing _____	big + est _____
sun + y _____	quit + ing _____
rot + en _____	**snow + y _____
**rain + ing _____	rob + er _____
*help + er _____	bright + en _____
fun + y _____	mad + er _____
**wool + en _____	*old + est _____
wed + ing _____	shop + ing _____
*fast + er _____	got + en _____
hot + est _____	flop + y _____
*trick + y _____	*jump + ing _____

➡ * Why don't you double the consonant in these words? _____

_____

➡ ** Why don't you double the consonant in these words? _____

_____

RULE

Drop-the-*e* Rule: When a root ends in a silent *e*, drop the *e* before adding a vowel suffix.

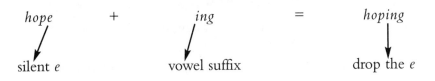

hope   +   *ing*   =   *hoping*

silent *e*   vowel suffix   drop the *e*

➡ Underline the first letter of the suffix. If it is a vowel, cross out the silent e in the root. Write the new word.

smil~~e~~	+	ing	*smiling*	large	+	er
froze	+	en		use	+	ful
care	+	less		dance	+	ing
smoke	+	y		take	+	en
sure	+	ly		style	+	ish
shine	+	ing		lone	+	ly
chose	+	en		shade	+	y
safe	+	ty		leave	+	ing
large	+	est		place	+	ment
write	+	ing		late	+	est
skate	+	er		change	+	ing
force	+	ful		wide	+	er
broke	+	en		ice	+	y

Proofing Practice

➡ Two common words are misspelled in each of the sentences below. Correct them as shown.

1.   *skating*
   We wanted to go ~~skateing~~ on the frozzen pond, but the park guard said that we had to wait for colder weather.

2. Nothing makes me mader than my dog's diging up my new plants.

3. My uncle is still useing a woulden tennis racket.

4. Rob was the yungest guest at the weding party.

The Drop-the-*e* Rule: When a root ends in a _____ e, drop the _____ before adding a _____ suffix *(hope + ing = hoping).*

➡ Add suffixes to the roots. Remember to apply the Drop-the-*e* Rule.

use	+	ing	_____	*wide	+	ly	_____
large	+	er	_____	broke	+	en	_____
*waste	+	ful	_____	spice	+	y	_____
bite	+	ing	_____	*age	+	less	_____
*amaze	+	ment	_____	blame	+	ed	_____
smoke	+	y	_____	ride	+	ing	_____
*safe	+	ly	_____	ice	+	y	_____

➡ * Why don't you drop the e from these words? _____

_____

➡ Add suffixes to these roots.

care	+	ing	_____	place	+	ing	_____
care	+	ful	_____	place	+	ment	_____
care	+	less	_____				
				safe	+	ly	_____
love	+	ly	_____	safe	+	est	_____
love	+	ing	_____	safe	+	ty	_____
love	+	er	_____	safe	+	ty	_____
large	+	er	_____	use	+	ing	_____
large	+	est	_____	use	+	ful	_____
large	+	ly	_____	use	+	er	_____

A vowel suffix _____ with a _____.

RULE

The Y Rule: When a root ends in *y*, change the *y* to *i* when adding a suffix (*easy + est = easiest; happy + ness = happiness*).

EXCEPTION

Keep the *y* if a vowel comes before it (*play + er = player; joy + ful = joyful*).
Keep the *y* if adding the suffix *-ing* (*cry + ing = crying; study + ing = studying*).

➤ Add suffixes or plural endings to the roots. Remember to apply the Y Rule. Circle any vowels that come just before y in the roots. Circle the *-ing* suffixes. Remember that these words will be exceptions to the Y Rule.

puppy	+	es	_____	crispy + er	_____
funny	+	est	_____	*play + ing	_____
*try	+	ing	_____	noisy + est	_____
easy	+	ly	_____	**joy + ful	_____
**buy	+	er	_____	lazy + er	_____
lady	+	es	_____	**pray + er	_____
**pay	+	ment	_____	sunny + er	_____
healthy	+	est	_____	easy + er	_____
party	+	es	_____	happy + ness	_____
pretty	+	est	_____	*study + ing	_____

➤ * Why don't you change the *y* to *i* in these words? _____

_____

➤ ** Why don't you change the *y* to *i* in these words? _____

_____

EXCEPTION

Shy becomes *shyly* and *shyness*.

21

The Doubling Rule: If a root has one s_____, ends in o_____ consonant, and has one v_____, double the final consonant before adding a v_____ suffix (*hop* —→ *hopping*).

The Drop-the-*e* Rule: When a root ends in a s_____ _____, drop the _____ before a v_____ suffix *(hope* —→ *hoping)*.

The Y Rule: When a root ends in a _____, change the _____ to _____ when adding a suffix *(easiest)*. Keep the *y* if a v_____ comes before it *(player)* or if adding _____ *(cry* —→ *crying)*.

→ For each word below, write the root and then write the name of the spelling rule used to form the word. If no rule was applied, write *none*.

	Root	Rule
shady	shade	drop-the-e
chosen		
bigger		
cleaner		
riding		
useful		
wealthier		
changing		
greatest		
funniest		
tasty		
using		
muddy		
fallen		
playing		
smiling		
larger		

➤ Your teacher will dictate words that have vowel suffixes. Spell them under the correct heading. Remember to apply the spelling rules.

-ing	*-y*	*-er*
_____	_____	_____
_____	_____	_____
_____	_____	_____

-est	*-en*	*-ish*
_____	_____
_____	_____
_____	_____

➤ Find and circle all of the words above in the puzzle below. The words can be found in a straight line across or up and down.

```
        ↓
B R I N G I N G W D H E W N A R E O R F O
I T S E L F I S H I B R O K E N A E A A N
G D S I N A S I I G L E O N T E S D I S S
G R W R I T I N G G O P D T H E I E N T U
E B E F O R E A H I D D E N D D E I Y E N
S N G I C Y A V E N O W N E L S R U F S N
T F I F A T T E R G X P R E T T I E S T Y
```

➤ Start at the arrow and write the leftover letters in the blanks below. Work from left to right.

＿ ＿ ＿ ＿ ＿   ＿ ＿ ＿ ＿   ＿ ＿ ＿ ＿   ＿ ＿   ＿   ＿ ＿ ＿ ＿ ＿ ＿

＿,   ＿ ＿ ＿ ＿   ＿ ＿ ＿   ＿   ＿ ＿ ＿ ＿ ＿   ＿ ＿ ＿ ＿ ＿ ＿   ＿

＿ ＿ ＿ ＿ ＿   ＿ ＿ ＿ ＿ ＿ ＿.

➤ What rule do the letters spell? The _____-_____-_____ Rule.

➡ Fill in each blank with one of these suffixes so that the sentences make sense. In the last four sentences you may need to add, drop, or change some letters.

-ing   *-er*   *-est*   *-ish*   *-y*   *-en*

1. Nathan is still pack_____ his trunk.

2. The old_____ woman I know is very health_____.

3. The stick_____ taffy will take time to hard_____.

4. Please hand me the wood_____ spoon so I can stir the beat_____ eggs.

5. My piece of cake is small_____ than yours. But Norman has the small_____ piece.

6. Will you help me length_____ my skirt? The styles are long_____ this year than they were last year.

7. It will be cloud_____, rain_____, and cold_____ this weekend.

8. Martin is clean_____ his mess_____ room.

9. Megan is play_____ by herself because she is self_____ with her toys.

10. Mr. Packer is luck_____ to be so health_____.

11. We are bank_____ at the near_____ bank.

12. It is fool_____ to go fish_____ in this wind_____ weather.

13. the roads were very ice_____ because last night's rain had froze_____.

14. Sally gave the baby the pretty_____ little wood_____ drum_____ boy I have ever seen.

15. Janet and Roberto were save_____ money for the wed_____.

16. I often feel like quit_____ my job at the wool_____ mill and going into farm_____.

<--------->   <--------->   <--------->
long   longer   longest

➤ Add the suffixes -er and -est to these roots. Fill in each blank with the word that makes sense in the sentence.

1. cold   People say that this winter will be _____ than last winter. In fact, this should be the _____ winter in years.

2. fast   The ostrich is the _____ running bird. It can certainly run _____ than a duck.

3. few   The object of the game is to make _____ mistakes than the other players. The one who makes the _____ mistakes wins.

4. bright The sun is the _____ object in our sky. The sun is _____ than the moon.

5. strong This coffee is _____ than I like it. But the Greasy Spoon Cafe has the _____ coffee I ever tried to drink.

6. sad   Ellen has the _____ look on her face. She looks _____ than I have ever seen her.

7. easy   My math test was _____ than my history test. But my English test was the _____ of all.

8. large   Tomako gave Ronald the _____ gift. It was even _____ than the one he gave her.

9. hot   The sun is _____ in Texas than it is in Kansas. But it is _____ in New Mexico.

10. early The _____ I can come is six o'clock. If I can make it _____, I will call.

11. mad   My mother can get much _____ than my father can. The _____ I've ever seen her is when I wrecked her car.

12. pretty I think that lilacs are the _____ spring flowers, but Justin thinks that tulips are _____.

➡ Read the following sentences and circle all the words from List 10 that you can find.

1. Irene has eaten the biggest piece of cake.

2. The younger boy with the curly hair is hanging his picture higher on the wall.

3. Hiro is skating on the frozen pond.

4. The sooner you do the dishes, the longer you will have for playing.

5. Ms. Harper was planting corn next to the wooden fence.

6. It gets darker faster in the months after the leaves have fallen.

7. The children will get dirty swinging and sliding in the muddy creek.

8. The icy roads made driving risky.

9. The foolish child was swimming in the deepest part of the pool.

10. It is windy and rainy today.

➡ Take out a piece of blank paper. Your teacher will dictate three of the sentences above for you to write.

➡ Now select ten words from List 10 and create a short story or a descriptive paragraph that uses those words. Be creative and avoid repetition!

Reading Accuracy: Demonstrate your accuracy in reading and spelling List 10 words. Your teacher will select ten words to read and ten practical spelling words for you to spell. Record your scores on the Accuracy Checklist. Work toward 90–100 percent accuracy.

Reading Proficiency: Now build up your reading fluency with List 10 words. Decide on your rate goal with your teacher. Record your progress on the Proficiency Graph.

My goal for reading List 10 is _____ words per minute with two or fewer errors.

LIST 11: THREE SOUNDS OF -ed*

/t/	/d/	/ed/	Mixed with Drop-the-*e* Rule	Mixed with Doubling and *Y* Rules
asked	called	acted	bored	begged
banked	crawled	added	cared	buried
barked	filled	crowded	carved	carried
brushed	filmed	drifted	caused	clapped
camped	formed	ended	chased	cried
dressed	formed	floated	closed	dried
dumped	happened	folded	created	dropped
fixed	learned	handed	danced	envied
forced	ordered	invented	fired	fried
helped	owned	landed	forced	grabbed
jumped	played	lasted	hired	hurried
kicked	pressed	lifted	joked	married
kissed	pulled	melted	loved	planned
knocked	rained	needed	named	robbed
laughed	rolled	painted	placed	shipped
licked	screamed	planted	raised	shopped
milked	seemed	pointed	saved	skinned
mixed	signed	punted	scared	snapped
packed	smelled	rented	served	spotted
passed	snowed	roasted	shaped	stepped
picked	spelled	rusted	skated	stopped
pumped	spilled	sounded	smiled	studied
rocked	stayed	started	supposed	tried
stamped	trained	tested	tasted	trimmed
stuffed	turned	treated	tired	tripped
thanked	used	twisted	typed	whipped
tricked	watered	waited	united	worried
washed	yelled	wanted	used	wrapped

*All words on this list are practical spelling words. The teacher and student should decide together how many of these words the student will be responsible for spelling.

★ The suffix -*ed* is added to verbs (action words) to place the action in the past. For example, "Today I <u>plant</u>; yesterday I <u>planted</u>." The suffix -*ed* can sound like /t/ as in *jumped*, /d/ as in *called*, or /əd/ as in *acted*.

➡ Circle and pronounce the root in the following words.

mixed	yelled	added	signed
watered	acted	brushed	wanted
floated	filmed	kissed	ordered
played	needed	asked	called

➡ Circle the suffix -*ed* in the following words. Be careful; what looks like a suffix may really be part of a root. You should have a complete word left over if you have circled a suffix.

asked	smelled	kissed	spelled
hundred	folded	bobsled	banked
filled	dumped	crowded	bled
ended	filmed	stamped	landed

➡ Fill in the blanks with the root or with the root and the suffix -*ed*.

wait   1. Today I _____; yesterday I _____.

fix   2. Today I _____ the car; yesterday I _____the car.

call   3. Today I _____; yesterday I _____.

help   4. Today I _____; yesterday I _____.

snow   5. Today it _____s; yesterday it _____.

➡ What sound does -ed have in the following words? Say the root first and then put it in the past tense. Say it aloud. Write /t/, /d/, or /əd/.

passed	/_____/	acted	/_____/	planted	/_____/
camped	/_____/	spilled	/_____/	rained	/_____/
landed	/_____/	picked	/_____/	crawled	/_____/
drifted	/_____/	smelled	/_____/	kissed	/_____/

➡ Your teacher will dictate some words. Repeat each word, isolate the root, and spell it. Then write the whole word.

Root	Copy	ABC Order
1. _____ + ed = _____		_____
2. _____ + ed = _____		_____
3. _____ + ed = _____		_____
4. _____ + ed = _____		_____
5. _____ + ed = _____		_____
6. _____ + ed = _____		_____
7. _____ + ed = _____		_____
8. _____ + ed = _____		_____
9. _____ + ed = _____		_____
10. _____ + ed = _____		_____

➡ Now go back and write the words in alphabetical order.

Review

The three sounds -ed can make are /_____/, /_____/, and /_____/.

★ The word *jumped* is pronounced /jumpt/.
The word *played* is pronounced /playd/.

➤ Spell the words below the way they should be spelled in the crossword puzzle.

/jumpt/ (1 Across)   /rockt/ (5 Across)   /seemd/ (8 Across)   /raind/ (5 Down)

/campt/ (6 Down)   /pickt/ (3 Down)   /orderd/ (10 Across)   /pulld/ (3 Across)

/pressd/ (9 Across)   /milkt/ (2 Down)   /calld/ (7 Across)   /farmd/ (4 Down)

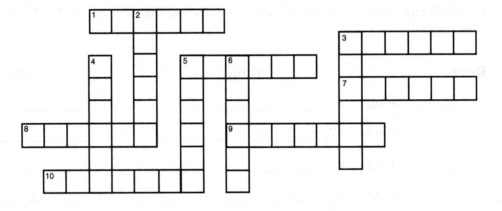

➤ Your teacher will dictate some words. Isolate and spell the suffix that you hear. Then write the whole word.

	Suffix	Copy	ABC Order
1. pump +	___ = ___		___
2. sad +	___ = ___		___
3. smell +	___ = ___		___
4. act +	___ = ___		___
5. fall +	___ = ___		___
6. play +	___ = ___		___
7. like +	___ = ___		___
8. wash +	___ = ___		___

➤ Now go back and write the words in alphabetical order.

★ If *-ed* has the /əd/ sound, it adds another syllable to the root *(add ⟶ added)*. If *-ed* has the /t/ or /d/ sound, it does not add another syllable *(talk ⟶ talked, call ⟶ called)*.

➡ Read the root and then the word with an –ed suffix. How many syllables are in the second word?

Today I . . .	Yesterday I . . .	Number of Syllables in the Second Word
cross	crossed	_____
film	filmed	_____
twist	twisted	_____
walk	walked	_____
pack	packed	_____
start	started	_____
wait	waited	_____
form	formed	_____
roast	roasted	_____
need	needed	_____

➡ Your teacher will dictate some words. Repeat the word; then say only the root. Spell the root. Then spell the suffix. Finally, spell the whole word.

Root	Suffix	Root + Suffix
1. _____	_____	_____
2. _____	_____	_____
3. _____	_____	_____
4. _____	_____	_____
5. _____	_____	_____
6. _____	_____	_____
7. _____	_____	_____
8. _____	_____	_____

➡️ Write these words in the correct column according to the sounds -ed makes.

fixed	yelled	lasted	chased	stepped
wanted	joined	mixed	named	skated
typed	boasted	wished	learned	rolled
tasted	signed	owned	added	bored
shopped	lifted	wrapped	needed	

-ed = /t/	*-ed = /d/*	*-ed = /əd/*
_____	_____	_____
_____	_____	_____
_____	_____	_____
_____	_____	_____
_____	_____	_____
_____	_____	_____
_____	_____	_____
_____	_____	_____

⭐ Now that you have practiced the three sounds of -ed, learn this fourth, not very common, sound:

-ed sometimes says /ēd/ as in *hurried, studied, envied*, and some other two-syllable words that end in *y* in the present tense *(hurry, study,* and *envy)*.

➡️ Write the past tense of these verbs and pronounce them as you write, remembering the /ēd/ sound.

bury_____   worry_____   study_____

marry_____   envy_____   hurry_____

carry_____

Review

The Doubling Rule: If a root has one syllable, ends in one consonant, and has one vowel, double the final consonant before adding a vowel suffix *(hop* ⟶ *hopping)*.

➡ Add the suffix *-ed* to these roots.

stop_____   wait_____   beg_____

wrap_____   skin_____   sign_____

ask_____   ship_____   plan_____

melt_____   trim_____   grab_____

Review

The Drop-the-e Rule: When a root ends in a silent *e*, drop the *e* before adding a vowel suffix *(hope* ⟶ *hoping)*.

➡ Add the suffix *-ed* to these roots.

use_____   love_____   smile_____

cause_____   bore_____   raise_____

dance_____   close_____   force_____

unite_____   suppose_____   tire_____

Review

The Y Rule: When a root ends in a *y*, change the *y* to *i* when adding a suffix *(easy* ⟶ *easiest)*. Keep the *y* if a vowel comes before it *(play* ⟶ *player)* or if you add *ing (cry* ⟶ *crying)*.

➡ Add the suffix *-ed* to these roots.

cry_____   carry_____   marry_____

worry_____   try_____   play_____

stay_____   study_____   fry_____

dry_____   envy_____   hurry_____

➡ For each word below, add the suffix *-ed*. Sometimes you will add only the suffix and other times you will have to apply the Doubling Rule, the Drop-the-*e* Rule, or the *Y* Rule. Check the procedure you need to follow for adding *-ed*. Then write the word.

	Add suffix with no changes	Doubling Rule	Drop-the-*e* Rule	*Y* Rule	
1. place + ed			✔		placed
2. clap + ed					
3. laugh + ed					
4. hurry + ed					
5. ship + ed					
6. save + ed					
7. trim + ed					
8. turn + ed					
9. happen + ed					
10. envy + ed					
11. suppose + ed					
12. bury + ed					
13. order + ed					
14. spot + ed					
15. skate + ed					
16. dry + ed					
17. whip + ed					
18. sign + ed					

➡ Add the suffix -*ed* to the following words. Think first; you may need to double the final consonant, drop a silent *e*, or change a *y* to *i*.

snap_____   study_____   rent_____   use_____

type_____   chase_____   save_____   want_____

snow_____   land_____   shop_____   rob_____

fry_____   tire_____   serve_____   bark_____

crawl_____   step_____   bury_____   need_____

➡ Fill in the blanks with words from above that make sense in the sentences.

1. I looked all over for an apartment that I could afford. I finally found one and

   _ _ _ _ _ _ it.

2. The dog _ _ _ _ _ _ the cat up into the tree.

3. Mai-Lin _ _ _ _ _ _ _ to buy a gift for her friend. She _ _ _ _ _ _ _ all day Saturday before she found what she wanted.

4. The turtle _ _ _ _ _ _ _ at me as I walked past it.

5. Martha wrote her paper and Gregory _ _ _ _ _ it for her.

6. It _ _ _ _ to upset Grandma when the dog _ _ _ _ _ _ _ .

7. The burglar _ _ _ _ _ _ the bank.

8. Although it had _ _ _ _ _ _ _ heavily, the pilot _ _ _ _ _ _ _ the plane safely.

9. Patrick put all his extra change in a bank. In a month, he had _ _ _ _ _ $15.00.

10. We _ _ _ _ _ _ _   _ _ _ _ _ _ eggs for breakfast.

11. Alan and Carter _ _ _ _ _ _ _ for the test until 11:00 p.m. Then they were so

    _ _ _ _ _ that they went to bed.

12. Sam _ _ _ _ _ _ three stitches and a shot after he _ _ _ _ _ _ _ on the rusty nail.

13. Fido _ _ _ _ _ _ _ under our fence and _ _ _ _ _ _ his bone in the neighbor's yard.

Proofing Practice

What is wrong in these sentences? Correct the spelling mistakes and rewrite the sentences. The number in parentheses tells you how many mistakes are in the sentence.

1. We planed to drive to the skateing rink. (2)

   _____

   _____

2. The whiped cream tasteed great on the fresh berrys. (3)

   _____

   _____

3. As I trimed the hedge, Dad mixxed up a batch of cookys. (3)

   _____

   _____

4. Judith triped on the sidewalk and droped all her shoping bags. (3)

   _____

   _____

5. Peter was supposd to meet us at 5:00; we worryed when he didn't come. (2)

   _____

   _____

6. The rober forct open the door, spoted the T.V. set, grabed it, and fled. (4)

   _____

   _____

7. The children formd a circle and then dancet around the tree. (2)

   _____

   _____

8. When Peter steped onto the icey sidewalk, he fell and skined his knee. (3)

   _____

   _____

➤ Read the following sentences and circle all the words from List 11 that you can find.

1. Alberto asked if it had rained or snowed there.

2. The children screamed and clapped their hands when the seal barked and then jumped through the hoop.

3. Toshi had typed the letter but hadn't signed it.

4. Emma tried to be brave, but she was still scared of the dark.

5. When the plane landed, the worried woman hurried to catch her next flight.

6. Justin washed his face, brushed his teeth, and got dressed for work.

7. The band played as the crowd danced to the lively music.

8. Lucy watered the garden after she planted it.

9. Mrs. Fineberg thanked everyone for the gift and then called her husband.

10. After the house was painted, Kelly wanted to plant roses in the flower bed.

➤ Take out a piece of blank paper. Your teacher will dictate three of the sentences above for you to write.

➤ Now select ten words from List 11 and create a short story or a descriptive paragraph that uses those words. Be creative and avoid repetition!

Reading Accuracy: Demonstrate your accuracy in reading and spelling List 11 words. Your teacher will select ten words to read and ten practical spelling words for you to spell. Record your scores on the Accuracy Checklist. Work toward 90–100 percent accuracy.

Reading Proficiency: Now build up your reading fluency with List 11 words. Decide on your rate goal with your teacher. Record your progress on the Proficiency Graph.

My goal for reading List 11 is _____ words per minute with two or fewer errors.

bated	hater	rated	snipper
batted	hatter	ratted	snipping
bidding	hidden	ridding	spiting
biding	hiding	riding	spitting
caning	* hoped	riper	* staring
canning	* hopped	ripper	starring
cuter	* hoping	robbed	stilled
cutter	* hopping	robed	striped
diner	mating	* scared	stripped
* dinner	matting	scarred	styled
doted	moping	scarring	taped
dotted	mopping	* scary	taping
filed	pined	scraper	tapped
* filled	pinned	scrapper	tapping
* filling	planed	sloping	wiled
filing	* planned	* sloppy	willed
griping	planing	sniper	
gripping	* planning	sniping	

*Practical spelling words. The teacher and student should decide together how many of these words the student will be responsible for spelling.

★ You will be able to spell troublesome word pairs such as *filed* and *filled* if you are able to tell whether the first syllable is open or closed.

Review

A closed syllable has only one vowel and ends in a consonant. The vowel sound is short *(căt, ĭf)*.
An open syllable ends in one vowel; the vowel is usually long *(lō, crā)*.

➡ Categorize the following syllables according to their vowel sounds. Pronounce each syllable as you write it.

tu	ro	dot	scrap	pla
tub	rob	do	scra	plan
mat	sni	ri	gri	hat
ma	snip	rid	grip	ha

Long-Vowel Sound   **Short-Vowel Sound**

_____   _____   _____   _____

_____   _____   _____   _____

_____   _____   _____   _____

_____   _____   _____   _____

_____   _____   _____   _____

➡ Your teacher will dictate some syllables. Repeat each syllable aloud as you spell it.

1. _____   5. _____   9. _____   13. _____

2. _____   6. _____   10. _____   14. _____

3. _____   7. _____   11. _____   15. _____

4. _____   8. _____   12. _____

➡️ Mark the vowel in the first syllable long or short. Pronounce the syllables and combine them to read the whole word.

mo	ping	moping
sni	per	sniper
cu	ter	cuter
dot	ted	dotted
hop	ping	hopping
spi	ting	spiting
hat	ter	hatter
bi	ding	biding

mop	ping	mopping
snip	per	snipper
cut	ter	cutter
do	ted	doted
ho	ping	hoping
spit	ting	spitting
ha	ter	hater
bid	ding	bidding

➡️ Pronounce the root. Then pronounce the past tense of the root. The suffix -ed does not add an extra syllable in these words because it has the sound of /t/ or /d/. Both the root and the past tense have only one syllable.

file	filed
rob	robbed
stripe	striped
scar	scarred
tape	taped

fill	filled
robe	robed
strip	stripped
scare	scared
tap	tapped

Review

Open and closed syllables.

1. An open syllable ends in one _____, which has a _____ sound.

2. A closed syllable has only one _____ and ends in a _____.

The vowel sound is _____.

➤ Your teacher will dictate some words. Repeat each word and identify the sound of the first vowel. If it is long, spell it in an open syllable, ending in a vowel. If the vowel is short, spell it in a closed syllable, ending in a consonant. Then write the whole word.

First Syllable	Copy	ABC Order
1. _____ + ping = _____		_____
2. _____ + ted = _____		_____
3. _____ + per = _____		_____
4. _____ + ting = _____		_____
5. _____ + ping = _____		_____
6. _____ + ner = _____		_____
7. _____ + ping = _____		_____
8. _____ + py = _____		_____
9. _____ + ted = _____		_____
10. _____ + ling = _____		_____

➤ Your teacher will pronounce some words. If you hear a long-vowel sound in the first syllable, fill in one missing consonant. If you hear a short-vowel sound, fill in two missing consonants.

	Copy	ABC Order
1. ri_____er	_____	_____
2. pla_____ing	_____	_____
3. gri_____ing	_____	_____
4. slo_____ing	_____	_____
5. ra_____ed	_____	_____
6. sta_____ing	_____	_____
7. pi_____ed	_____	_____
8. hi_____ing	_____	_____
9. ho_____ed	_____	_____
10. pi_____ed	_____	_____

➤ Now go back and write the words in each section in alphabetical order.

★ If a word has a double consonant after the first vowel, the vowel is short, and the root can be seen in the word. In *hopping, hop* is the root.

If a word has a single consonant after the first vowel, the vowel is long, and the root has dropped the silent e because a vowel suffix was added. In *hoping, hope* is the root.

➡ Write the root in each of the following words and then pronounce the words aloud.

planned_____ *planed_____ spitting_____ spiting_____

ridding_____ *riding_____ *ratted_____ *rated_____

sniper_____ snipper_____ cuter_____ *cutter_____

tapping_____ *taping_____ filled_____ filed_____

ripper_____ *riper_____ mating_____ matting_____

sloppy_____ sloping_____ canning_____ *caning_____

dotted_____ *doted_____ batted_____ *bated_____

➡ Complete the puzzle with the starred words above.

Across
1. made level
3. more ready to eat
5. used to cut something
7. reduced force (with____breath)
8. recording on tape

Down
2. showed too much fondness (____on her pet)
3. sitting on a moving animal
4. told or informed on
5. weaving with cane
6. regarded; graded

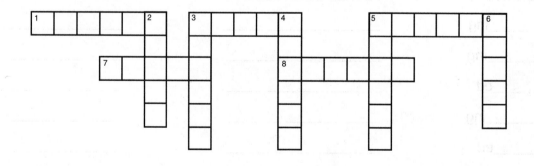

➡ Circle the middle consonant or consonants in the following words. Then write the words in the correct column.

filed	tapped	pined	stripped	wiled
filled	taped	pinned	striped	willed
robbed	riper	moped	starring	
robed	ripper	mopped	staring	

Long-Vowel Words **(Single Middle Consonant)**	**Short-Vowel or *r*-Controlled Words** **(Double Middle Consonant)**
_____ _____	_____ _____
_____ _____	_____ _____
_____ _____	_____ _____
_____ _____	_____ _____

➡ Your teacher will dictate some words. Spell them under the correct heading.

Long-Vowel Words **(Single Middle Consonant)**	**Short-Vowel or *r*-Controlled Words** **(Double Middle Consonant)**
_____ _____	_____ _____
_____ _____	_____ _____
_____ _____	_____ _____

Proofing Practice

Two common words are misspelled in each of the sentences below. Correct them as shown.

1. Janet was ~~planing~~ *planning* on wearing the new doted dress.

2. My father is gripping about the way I am always taping my feet under the table.

3. Do we have to have caned peas for diner again?

4. My baby brother is a very slopy eater; he is always spiting up his food.

➡ Decide which root makes sense in each blank in the sentences below. Then add the suffix *-ing, -er,* or *-ed* and spell the word correctly in the blank.

1. grip   Rachel _____ the dashboard as

   gripe   she _____ about my driving.

2. scare   Are you _____ that you will be_____

   scar   from the accident?

3. mope   I was mad that I had to work, so I _____ the whole time I

   mop   _____ the floors.

4. tap   Adam was _____ his foot to the music as he

   tape   _____ it on his tape recorder.

5. pine   The girl was_____ away for the person in the picture that she

   pin   had _____ to the wall.

6. file   I _____ my nails while the attendant

   fill   _____ my gas tank.

7. hop   Diana _____she would get a chance to see the rabbits

   hope   as they _____ into the woods.

8. robe   The _____ burglar was the one who

   rob   _____ the bank.

9. strip   The painters _____ the _____ wall-

   stripe paper off the living room walls.

10. ripe   Maria _____ her jacket when she reached for the apple

    rip   that looked _____ than the one she already had.

11. stare The fans were all _____ at the teenage idol who

    star   _____ in the new movie.

➡ Read the following sentences and circle all the words from List 12 that you can find.

1. The striped cat was staring at the scared rat.

2. Roger filed the last of the letters before filling the coffee pot with water.

3. The Lennon family had dinner last night at the local diner.

4. Use the rubber scraper to clean out the sloppy mess in the bowl.

5. The class listened with bated breath as Casper told a scary ghost story.

6. I gripped my purse as I lightly tapped on the door.

7. Kathy was hoping to get her hair cut and styled today.

8. The diner had striped walls and dotted floors.

9. This movie with the tubby panda has been rated the best of the year.

10. Chris Carson was canning only the riper peaches.

11. Henry filed his nails after he mopped the kitchen floor.

➡ Take out a piece of blank paper. Your teacher will dictate three of the sentences above for you to write.

➡ Now select ten words from List 12 and create a short story or a descriptive paragraph that uses those words. Be creative and avoid repetition!

Reading Accuracy: Demonstrate your accuracy in reading and spelling List 12 words. Your teacher will select ten words to read and ten practical spelling words for you to spell. Record your scores on the Accuracy Checklist. Work toward 90–100 percent accuracy.

Reading Proficiency: Now build up your reading fluency with List 12 words. Decide on your rate goal with your teacher. Record your progress on the Proficiency Graph.

My goal for reading List 12 is _____ words per minute with two or fewer errors.

LIST 13: COMMON PREFIXES

re-	de-	sub-	pre-	un-	ex-
* rebuild	* decide	* subject	* prepare	* unable	* exact
* receive	* defeat	* subtract	* present	* unfair	* exam
* recess	* defend	sublet	* present	* unfinished	* except
* recite	* delight	submarine	predict	* unfriendly	* exchange
* record	* department	submerge	prefer	* unkind	* excite
* refuse	* depend	submit	prefix	* unknown	* excuse
* rejoice	* deposit	subscribe	prenatal	unborn	* exit
* remain	* describe	subsist	prepaid		* expect
* remind	* deserve	subsoil	preschool	**in-**	* explain
* remove	* desire	substance	prescribe	* income	* explore
* repair	* destroy	subway	preside	* inform	* express
* repeat	debate	subzero	pretend	* inside	* extra
* repel	decrease		preview	* insult	exceed
* report	defect			* intend	exclude
* respect	defer	**pro-**	**per-**	* invent	exempt
* return	deform	* produce	* perfect	inboard	exhaust
* review	degrade	* program	* perfume	incorrect	exist
* reward	demand	* project	* perhaps	increase	expand
recall	demote	* promise	* permit	indent	expel
refill	depart	* protect	perform	indirect	expert
reform	depress	proceed	perplex	inept	expire
refresh	descend	proclaim	persist	inflate	explode
refuel		product	perspire	inhale	export
regain		profile	persuade	inscribe	expose
regard		profit	pertain	insert	extend
reject		progress	perturb	insist	extreme
resist		promote	peruse	inspect	
		propel	pervade	inspire	
		prospect		intake	
		prosper			
		provide			

*Practical spelling words. The teacher and student should decide together how many of these words the student will be responsible for spelling.

★ A **prefix** is a word part that comes before a root and changes its meaning or forms a new word (*unpaid*, *prepaid*, *decrease*, *increase*).

A root is not always a complete word by itself. It may come from Latin, Greek, or Anglo-Saxon (*propel*, *prefer*).

➡ Study these List 13 prefixes and their meanings.

re-	=	back, again	sub-	=	below, under
de-	=	down, away from	pre-	=	before
in-	=	not, in	pro-	=	forward
un-	=	not	per-	=	through, completely
ex-	=	out			

➡ Circle the prefixes in the following words and write them after the word.

(re)call	*re*	unable	_____	extend	_____
prepare	_____	subway	_____	perfect	_____
indirect	_____	insane	_____	exit	_____
progress	_____	prefer	_____	unkind	_____
propel	_____	reform	_____	submarine	_____
perform	_____	depress	_____	debate	_____

➡ Now write the meaning of each prefix.

pre- = _____   re- = _____

pro- = _____   in- = _____

per- = _____   un- = _____

sub- = _____   de- = _____

ex- = _____

➤ Match each prefix with its meaning by writing the correct prefix in each blank.

re-   de-   sub-   ex-   pre-   per-   un-   in-   pro-

1. _____through, completely

2. _____down, away from

3. _____not, in

4. _____back, again

5. _____before

6. _____below, under

7. _____forward

8. _____not

9. _____out

➤ The following words contain prefixes. The meaning of the prefixes will help you complete the meaning of the words.

1. unable = _____able

2. intake = take_____

3. refill = fill_____

4. return = turn_____

5. depress = press_____

6. prepaid = paid_____

7. exit = go_____

8. unfair = _____fair

9. rebuild = build_____

10. indirect = _____direct

11. subsoil = _____the topsoil

12. preschool = _____school

13. unborn = _____yet born

14. incorrect = _____correct

15. subzero = _____zero

16. subway = travels_____ground

17. unkind = _____kind

18. unfriendly = _____friendly

19. export = send_____

20. proceed = move_____

Review

A _____ is a word part that comes before a root and changes its meaning or forms a new word.

A _____ is a word part that comes at the end of a root.

A _____ is the main word part to which prefixes and suffixes are attached.

➤ Circle and pronounce the prefixes in these words. Be careful; some words do not have prefixes. You should circle twenty prefixes.

(ex)press	unable	dictate	depart
submerge	pollute	perform	unfair
bonfire	prospect	prepare	indent
report	inflate	practice	punish
promote	excuse	dragon	refuel
degrade	persist	substance	perfume
except	submit	create	subtract

➤ Match each prefix with a root to make a real word. Then say the word as you write it.

sub	crease	_____	de	plain	_____
pre	crease	_____	in	stroy	_____
in	ject	*subject*	ex	fair	_____
de	dict	_____	un	sist	_____
ex	pect	_____	pro	vide	_____
in	spect	_____	pre	sist	_____
de	spect	_____	pro	pare	_____
re	part	_____	per	tect	_____

➤ Reorder the syllables to make a recognizable word. It will be easier if you circle the prefix and underline the suffix.

un	ly	friend	_____
vent	in	ed	_____
ex	ing	pect	_____
ing	ceed	pro	_____

➡ Isolate, pronounce, and spell the prefix you hear in the words dictated by your teacher. Then spell the whole word, saying it as you write.

Prefix	Word	ABC Order
Example: ___sub___ject	_subject_____	_____
1. _____ceed	_____	_____
2. _____cuse	_____	_____
3. _____paid	_____	_____
4. _____spect	_____	_____
5. _____hale	_____	_____
6. _____able	_____	_____
7. _____stance	_____	_____
8. _____scend	_____	_____
9. _____clude	_____	_____
10. _____suade	_____	_____

➡ Isolate, pronounce, and spell the root in the words dictated by your teacher. Then spell the whole word, saying it as you write.

Root	Word	ABC Order
Example: ex_pect_____	_expect_____	_____
11. in_____	_____	_____
12. per_____	_____	_____
13. sub_____	_____	_____
14. pre_____	_____	_____
15. pro_____	_____	_____
16. ex_____	_____	_____
17. de_____	_____	_____
18. re_____	_____	_____
19. ex_____	_____	_____
20. per_____	_____	_____

➡ Now go back and write the words in each section in alphabetical order.

→ Fill in the blanks with the correct prefixes. You may refer to the word list. Then write the words in the puzzle.

1. to go away = _____part (1 Down)

2. to put in = _____sert (10 Across)

3. to get again = _____gain (7 Across)

4. to carry out of the country =

   _____port (16 Across)

5. to move forward = _____gress
   (15 Across)

6. to go down in value = _____crease
   (13 Across)

7. not fit or able = _____ept (10 Down)

8. not helpful or nice = _____kind
   (2 Down)

9. to go forward = _____ceed (5 Down)

10. to choose before another = _____fer
    (9 Down)

11. to refuse to stop = _____sist
    (11 Down)

12. to put back = _____turn (14 Down)

13. to disturb completely = _____turb
    (17 Across)

14. act of taking in = _____take
    (4 Down)

15. to call out a feeling = _____cite
    (6 Down)

16. to say in front of others = _____claim
    (9 Across)

17. not fair = _____fair (2 Across)

18. under someone's powers = _____ject
    (8 Down)

19. to blow into = _____flate (3 Down)

20. very far out = _____treme (12 Across)

★ Students often confuse the prefixes *pre-* and *per-*. It will help you in spelling if you remember the meanings of these two prefixes:

pre- means "before"; *per-* means "through" or "completely."

➡ Fill in the blanks with *pre-* or *per-* and write the whole word. Then copy the words under the correct heading below.

1. to tell beforehand _____dict _____

2. to go through or do _____form _____

3. completely skilled; faultless _____fect _____

4. before birth _____natal _____

5. to put before _____fix _____

6. to continue completely; refuse to stop _____sist _____

7. to see beforehand _____view _____

8. to confuse completely; to puzzle _____plex _____

9. to pay beforehand _____pay _____

10. to spread throughout _____vade _____

11. to keep from happening _____vent _____

12. to read thoroughly _____use _____

13. to convince completely; to urge _____suade _____

14. to get ready beforehand _____pare _____

        pre- **Words**   *per-* **Words**

_____ _____   _____ _____

_____ _____   _____ _____

_____ _____   _____ _____

_____   _____

⭐ Most two-syllable words are accented on the first syllable *(fi´ nal, stu´ dent, hop´ ping)*. However, the accent pattern changes in two-syllable words that have a prefix in the first syllable and a root in the second syllable. We usually accent the root (con *fuse´*, ex *tend´*, pre *fer´*).

➡ Draw a box around the accented root in the following words and mark the accented vowel. Cross out silent letters. Then pronounce and combine the syllables.

sub⬚mĭt⬚	re⬚pēat⬚	expand	promote	unknown
inspect	propel	preside	explode	subsist
exempt	inflate	refuse	subscribe	demand
respect	express	decrease	reject	intend
perhaps	demote	exact	sublet	pervade
predict	subtract	persist	depend	inspire
excuse	proceed	prepay	perplex	insult

➡ In a few words, the prefix is accented. Draw a box around the accented prefix in the following words and mark the accented vowel. Notice that the prefix *pro-* can be pronounced two ways: /prō/ and /prŏ/, depending on the syllabication. The first syllable of *prospect* is *pros*; thus, the vowel is short. The first syllable of *program* is *pro*; thus, the vowel is long.

⬚prŏs⬚pect	⬚prō⬚gram	product	income	project
profit	profile	intake	promise	prosper
produce	inboard	subway	substance	subsoil

pro- says /prō/ in: *pro-* says /prŏ/ in:

_____   _____   _____

_____   _____   _____

_____   _____   _____

★ Some words can be used both as nouns (naming words) and as verbs (action words).
When the word is a noun, accent the prefix *(sub´ject)*.
When the word is a verb, accent the root *(sub ject´)*.

➡ Draw a box around the accented syllable and mark the accented vowel. Then pronounce and combine the syllables.

Nouns	Verbs	Nouns	Verbs
rē̄cess	recĕss	insult	insult
record*	record	present*	present
produce	produce	permit	permit
project*	project	reject	reject
progress*	progress		

➡ Read these sentences aloud. If the italicized word is a noun, draw a box around the prefix to show that it is accented. If it is a verb, draw a box around the root to show that it is accented.

1. The farmer had fresh *produce* for sale.   The school will *produce* a play.

2. I gave Judith a birthday *present.*   *Present* your report to the class.

3. Ms. Trabin will not *permit* smoking in her house.   You must get a driver's *permit.*

4. Martha completed her science *project.*   *Project* your voice so that we can hear you more clearly.

5. Peter *insulted* his partner.   Do not add *insult* to injury.

6. What is your best *subject* in school?   Rome *subjected* all of Greece to her rule.

7. We *progress* in learning, step by step.   Donald made good *progress* in reading.

8. Janis bought another *record* at the music store.   *Record* your progress on the Proficiency Graph.

*Syllabication differs in some words, depending on whether the word is a noun or a verb.

➡ Directions:
1. Your teacher will dictate a word with a prefix.
2. Repeat the word.
3. Isolate and pronounce the prefix, saying the sounds as you spell it in the first box.
4. Isolate and pronounce the root, saying the sounds as you spell it in the second box.
5. Write the whole word on the line, saying the sounds as you spell.

1. ☐ ☐ _____

2. ☐ ☐ _____

3. ☐ ☐ _____

4. ☐ ☐ _____

5. ☐ ☐ _____

6. ☐ ☐ _____

7. ☐ ☐ _____

8. ☐ ☐ _____

9. ☐ ☐ _____

10. ☐ ☐ _____

Proofing Practice

Two common words are misspelled in each of the sentences below. Correct them as shown.

reward
1. There will be a ~~reword~~ for the student who can subtrackt best.

2. Please explane why you would like to exschange this shirt.

3. We could repare it insted of replacing it.

4. The class desided to visit the Tomb of the Unnown Soldier.

★ Many English words contain Latin roots that are not real words by themselves. When these roots are combined with a prefix, they form a real word. The meanings of the Latin roots are often a clue to the meanings of the English words.

➡ Write the Latin roots next to the prefixes and read each word aloud.

pel = "to drive"	**spire = "to breathe"**
ex_____	in_____
re_____	*ex_____
pro_____	per_____
form = "to form"	**sist = "to stand"**
re_____	per_____
de_____	re_____
in_____	in_____
per_____	sub_____

➡ Complete the words by adding a prefix so that each sentence makes sense.

1. You can _____ pel a boat by using oars.

2. The boy promised to _____ form if given a second chance.

3. Most people _____ spire easily during the hot summer months.

4. I could not _____ sist tasting the frosting on the cake.

5. Shoes that are too tight will _____ form the feet.

6. The speaker _____ spired the crowd.

7. You must renew your license when your old one _____ pires.

8. The land was so poor that the farmers could barely _____ sist on it.

9. The teacher _____ sisted that the students complete their homework.

10. If students break the rules, they may be _____ pelled from school.

11. Please _____ form Nathan about the party.

*Drop the *s* to avoid a double /s/ sound.

➡ The Latin root *spect* means "to see" or "to look." Study these words, circle the roots, and underline the prefixes.

inspect   respect   *expect

➡ The Latin root *fect* means "to make" or "to do." Study these words, circle the roots, and underline the prefixes.

defect   perfect

➡ The Latin root *scribe* means "to write." Study these words, circle the roots, and underline the prefixes.

inscribe   subscribe   describe   prescribe

➡ The Latin root *tain* (from *tenere*) means "to hold" or "to keep." Study these words, circle the roots, and underline the prefixes.

detain   retain

➡ Read the following sentences and fill in the blanks with words from above that complete the sentences. The underlined words are your clues.

1. A doctor who <u>writes</u> down a treatment <u>before</u> you follow it,_____s medical advice.

2. The police <u>kept</u> the suspected thief from going <u>away</u>. They _____ed him.

3. When you <u>look out</u> for something, you _____ it to happen.

4. If you <u>write</u> your name <u>underneath</u> a statement, that means you _____, or agree, to the statement.

5. A police officer who <u>looks into</u> the facts of a crime _____s the evidence.

6. Work that is <u>done completely</u> and correctly is _____.

7. A person to whom you are willing <u>to look again</u> for advice is a person whom you

   _____.

8. A jeweler who <u>writes</u> your wedding date in your wedding ring _____s the date.

9. Sponges can absorb and _____ a lot of water.

*We drop the *s* in *spect* to avoid a double /s/ sound.

➡ Fill in the blanks with a word from the list below. Circle the word that gives you a clue about the prefix.

1. A motor that is (inside) a boat is called an __i n b o a r d__ motor.

2. The _ _ _ _ _ _ _ _ _ stayed under the water for a month.

3. Someone who can tell before it happens that it will rain can _ _ _ _ _ _ _ the weather.

4. Soil that is under the topsoil is called the _ _ _ _ _ _ _.

5. When you are tired out, you are _ _ _ _ _ _ _ed.

6. To plead or convince completely through reason or emotion is to

   _ _ _ _ _ _ _ _.

7. Percy choked when he _ _ _ _ _ _d, or breathed in, the thick smoke.

8. When you put something under water, you _ _ _ _ _ _ _ _ it.

9. It is proper to _ _ _ _ _ _, or stretch out, your hand when you meet someone.

10. When you go down the stairs, you _ _ _ _ _ _ _ them.

11. I wish prices would go down, or _ _ _ _ _ _ _ _.

12. If you leave someone out of your plans, you _ _ _ _ _ _ _ them.

13. I don't want to say the directions again; please do not ask me to _ _ _ _ _ _ them.

14. Our French teacher always has us say back what she says. She thinks that it is helpful

    for us to _ _ _ _ _ _ the lesson.

descend	exclude	persuade	predict
subsoil	exhaust	inhale	repeat
~~submerge~~	recite	decrease	submarine
inboard	extend		

➡ Read the following sentences and circle all the List 13 words that you can find.

1. Ms. Maxwell intends to present another report on the subject today.

2. We expect them to explain the new program at the department meeting.

3. I am unable to prepare my income tax return without your help.

4. Perhaps if we persist, we can prevent the government's destroying the records.

5. Subtract these two numbers from your gross income and then record your answer.

6. Remind me to untie my dirty shoes and remove them before I go inside.

7. When the unfriendly shopper returned the broken tape deck, he insulted the salesperson.

8. The teacher would not permit the children to go to recess if their work was unfinished.

9. You deserve a reward for informing us about the robbery.

10. The members can prevent unkind words if they show more respect for each other.

11. Let's explore some more places before we decide whether to rebuild the cabin here.

➡ Take out a piece of blank paper. Your teacher will dictate three of the sentences above for you to write.

➡ Now select ten words from List 13 and create a short story or a descriptive paragraph that uses those words. Be creative and avoid repetition!

Reading Accuracy: Demonstrate your accuracy in reading and spelling List 13 words. Your teacher will select ten words to read and ten practical spelling words for you to spell. Record your scores on the Accuracy Checklist. Work toward 90–100 percent accuracy.

Reading Proficiency: Now build up your reading fluency with List 13 words. Decide on your rate goal with your teacher. Record your progress on the Proficiency Graph.

My goal for reading List 13 is _____ words per minute with two or fewer errors.

LIST 14: ADDITIONAL COMMON PREFIXES

a–	dis–	ad–	ab–	ob–
* about	* discover	* address	* absent	* object
* above	* disease	* admire	abduct	oblong
* across	* dislike	adapt	abhor	obscene
* afar	* dismiss	addict	abort	obscure
* ahead	* distant	adept	absolve	observe
* alive	disabled	adhere	absorb	obsess
* aloud	discard	adjoin	abstain	obstruct
* among	disclose	adjust	abstract	obtain
* asleep	discount	admit	absurd	obtuse
* awake	discuss	advance		
* awhile	disgrace		**con–**	**inter–**
aback	disgust	**trans–**	* conclude	* interest
aboard	disperse	* transport	* conduct	* interrupt
adrift	distract	transact	* connect	interact
afire		transcend	* contain	intercede
afloat	**mis–**	transcribe	* contest	interchange
agree	* mischief	transfer	* control	interface
alert	* misspell	transform	confer	interfere
aloof	* mistake	translate	confess	interject
arise	misgive	transmit	confuse	interlock
ashore	mislead	transplant	consist	interlude
aside	mismatch		conspire	intersect
await	misplace		consult	
	misprint		contract	
	misquote		convict	
			convince	

*Practical spelling words. The teacher and student should decide together how many of these words the student will be responsible for spelling.

Review

A **prefix** is a word part that comes before a root and changes its meaning or forms a new word (*unpaid*, *prepaid*, *decrease*, *increase*).

A root is not always a complete word by itself. It may come from Latin, Greek, or Anglo-Saxon (*propel*, *prefer*).

➡ Study these wordlist prefixes and their meanings.

a-	=	on, in	trans-	=	across
ad-	=	to, toward	inter-	=	between, among
ab-	=	away from	con-	=	together, with
ob-	=	near, against, in the way	mis-	=	bad, wrong
dis-	=	opposite of, apart			

➡ Circle the prefixes in the following words and write them after the word.

ⓐlert_____ *a*_____	absent_____	interval_____
object_____	interstate_____	disgust_____
across_____	discuss_____	conference_____
adverb_____	confuse_____	advance_____
obtain_____	transform_____	transfer_____
absurd_____	mistake_____	misplace_____
awake_____	observe_____	translate_____
admire_____	conspire_____	interface_____
absorb_____	discover_____	disgrace_____

➡ Now write the meaning of each prefix.

dis- = _____   trans- = _____

ob- = _____   inter- = _____

a- = _____   mis- = _____

ad- = _____   con- = _____

ab- = _____

61

➡ Match each prefix with its meaning by writing the correct prefix in each blank.

a-   dis-   mis-   ad-   ob-   trans-   inter-   con-   ab-

1. _____ across

2. _____ together, with

3. _____ apart, opposite of

4. _____ between, among

5. _____ on, in

6. _____ to, toward

7. _____ away from

8. _____ wrong, bad

9. _____ against, in the way, near

➡ The following words contain prefixes. The meaning of the prefixes will help you complete the meaning of the words.

1. connect = join _____

2. disabled = _____ able

3. misplace = put in the _____ place

4. interstate = _____ states

5. misspell = spell _____

6. absent = _____ class

7. advance = move _____ a goal

8. adjoin = join _____

9. dislike = _____ like

10. object = argue _____

11. transmit = send _____

12. away = _____ the way

➡ Find and circle the twelve words above in the puzzle below. The words can be found in a straight line across or up and down.

T	C	H	E	P	M	R	A	D	V	A	N	C	E	E
D	O	F	I	M	I	S	S	P	E	L	L	X	I	N
I	N	T	E	R	S	T	A	T	E	T	E	R	M	E
S	N	A	A	N	P	S	B	E	T	O	W	E	E	N
A	E	D	I	S	L	I	K	E	A	B	S	E	N	T
B	C	J	A	W	A	Y	O	R	A	J	M	O	N	G
L	T	O	O	B	C	M	E	A	N	E	S	A	G	A
E	I	I	N	S	E	T	C	O	N	C	M	E	A	N
D	S	N	T	R	A	N	S	M	I	T	W	I	T	H

Start at the arrow and write the leftover letters in the blanks below. Work from left to right.

__ __ __   __ __ __ __ __

__ __ __ __   __ __ __

" __ __ __ __ __ "

" __ __ __ __ __ __ __   __ __

__ __ __ __ __ ."   __ __

__ __ __ __ __

" __ __ __ __ "   __ __ __ __ __ __

__ __ __ __ __   " __ __ __ ."

➡ Find and circle eighteen prefixes in the puzzle below. The prefixes can be found in a straight line across or up and down.

```
D O B D T A S
I N T E R E U
S P R O A B B
N R C O N U A
E E M I S N I
X A D P E R N
```

➡ Match each prefix with a root to make a real word. Then say the word as you write it.

inter	cert	_____		ad	sleep	_____
con	sorb	_____		mis	fer	_____
ab	lert	_____		trans	lead	_____
a	lock	_____		a	dress	_____
dis	ject	_____		mis	test	_____
ad	count	_____		trans	take	_____
trans	vance	_____		con	mire	_____
ob	plant	_____		ad	form	_____

➡ Reorder the word parts to make a recognizable word. It will be easier if you circle the prefix and underline the suffix.

struct	ob	ing	_____
dis	ed	miss	_____
gree	a	ing	_____
sorb	er	ab	_____
tain	ob	ed	_____
ed	dis	tract	_____

➤ Isolate, pronounce, and spell the prefix you hear in the words dictated by your teacher. Then write the whole word, saying it aloud as you spell.

Prefix	Copy	ABC Order
1. _____place	_____	_____
2. _____fer	_____	_____
3. _____rupt	_____	_____
4. _____spire	_____	_____
5 _____rupt	_____	_____
6. _____serve	_____	_____
7. _____ware	_____	_____
8. _____agree	_____	_____
9. _____dress	_____	_____
10. _____duct	_____	_____

➤ Isolate, pronounce, and spell the root in the words dictated by your teacher. Then write the whole word, saying it aloud as you spell.

Root	Copy	ABC Order
11. a_____	_____	_____
12. trans_____	_____	_____
13. con_____	_____	_____
14. ab_____	_____	_____
15. dis_____	_____	_____
16. ad_____	_____	_____
17. ob_____	_____	_____
18. mis_____	_____	_____
19. dis_____	_____	_____
20. ad_____	_____	_____

➤ Now go back and write the words in each section in alphabetical order.

➡ Fill in the blanks with the correct prefixes. You may refer to the word list. Then write each word in the puzzle.

1. to stick to = _____ here (11 Across)

2. going across = _____it (8 Down)

3. to lead in the wrong direction =

    _____lead (5 Down)

4. to scatter into parts = _____perse
    (3 Across)

5. to stop from doing = _____stain (10 Across)

6. to put together = _____ nect
    (7 Down)

7. to fit to = _____apt (13 Across)

8. to build with = _____struct
    (7 Across)

9. to give wrong information =

    _____ inform (9 Across)

10. to cross to a higher level =

    _____cend (12 Across)

11. to break apart = _____rupt
    (6 Down)

12. on or in the boat = _____board
    (4 Down)

13. to agree with = _____ sent
    (2 Down)

14. to melt apart = _____ solve
    (1 Down)

15. on fire = _____ fire (10 Down)

16. to thrust apart = _____ pel
    (1 Across)

➡ Draw a box around the accented root in the following words and mark the accented vowel. Then pronounce and combine the syllables.

con‾fuse‾	aboard	transact	consult
adept	adjoin	conspire	mislead
transact	disease	interfere	asleep
alarm	convince	admire	distract
observe	interrupt	afloat	adhere
misspell	absurd	discuss	absorb
intersect	contain	transcribe	disgust
connect	awake	mistake	obsess

➡ In a few words, the prefix is accented. Draw a box around the accented prefix in the following words and mark the accented vowel. Notice that only the first syllable of the prefix *inter-* is accented.

ĭnterest	interlude	distant	mischief	oblong

WORKSHEET 14-G

Review

If a word can function as both a noun and a verb, the noun form has the accent on the

_____ syllable *(sub´ject)* and the verb form has the accent on the

_____ syllable *(sub ject´)*.

➡ Draw a box around the accented syllable and mark the accented vowel. Then pronounce and combine the syllables.

Nouns	Verbs	Nouns	Verbs
trăns plant	trans plănt	contest	contest
transfer	transfer	contract	contract
transport	transport	convict	convict
addict	addict	conduct	conduct
address	address	object	object
misprint	misprint	discount	discount

➡ Read these sentences aloud. If the italicized word is a noun, draw a box around the prefix and accent it. If it is a verb, draw a box around the root and accent it.

1. Sign the con tract on the bottom line.

Muscles expand and *con tract.*

2. Don't forget to include your return *address.*

Please *address* these envelopes.

3. The jury *convicted* him of murder.

The *convict* escaped from prison.

4. What is the *object* of the game?

Many people *object* to loud music.

5. The woman *contested* the case.

Who won the *contest?*

6. The drug *addict* went to a clinic for treatment.

Some people are *addicted* to coffee.

7. You will need to get a *transfer* from the bus driver.

Transfer $50.00 to my checking account.

8. Ms. Carter will *conduct* the band.

The children's *conduct* was perfect.

➡ Directions:
1. Your teacher will dictate a word with a prefix.
2. Repeat the word.
3. Isolate and pronounce the prefix, saying the sounds as you spell it in the first box.
4. Isolate and pronounce the root, saying the sounds as you spell it in the second box.
5. Write the whole word on the line, saying the sounds as you spell.

1. ☐ ☐ _____

2. ☐ ☐ _____

3. ☐ ☐ _____

4. ☐ ☐ _____

5. ☐ ☐ _____

6. ☐ ☐ _____

7. ☐ ☐ _____

8. ☐ ☐ _____

9. ☐ ☐ _____

10. ☐ ☐ _____

Proofing Practice

Two common words are misspelled in each of the sentences below. Correct them as shown.

1. The letter was returned because there was a ~~mistaok~~ *mistake* in the adress.

2. I hope you do not objekt to my going ahed.

3. One way to avoid mispelling words is to say them alloud as you spell.

4. We can controll the diseaze through drug treatments.

★ Many English words contain Latin roots that are not real words by themselves. Combined with a prefix, these roots are often a clue to the meanings of the English words.

port means "to carry;" *duct* means "to lead;" *tain* means "to hold."

➡ Use the meanings of the Latin roots listed above and your knowledge of what prefixes mean to match the words to their definitions.

1. _____	to carry goods out of a country	transport
2. _____	to carry goods into a country	export
3. _____	one who carries news back	deport
4. _____	to carry across	reporter
5. _____	to carry away forcefully from a country	import[1]
6. _____	to admit a person as a member	conduct
7. _____	to lead or direct people together	product
8. _____	to lead someone away by force	induct
9. _____	something led forth; the result	deduct
10. _____	to lead or take away from	abduct
11. _____	to hold back; to keep from going	contain
12. _____	to hold something together	abstain[2]
13. _____	to hold yourself away from something	retain
14. _____	to get; to hold something near to you	detain
15. _____	to continue to hold in your mind	obtain

➡ Complete the words by adding a prefix so that the sentence makes sense.

16. This milk carton _____tains a gallon of milk.

17. My mother can _____duct her travel expenses from her income tax.

18. This perfume is _____ported1 from France.

19. To lose weight, you should _____tain[2] from eating sweets.

20. The United States _____ports wheat to other countries.

[1]Note that *n* changes to *m* in this word.
[2]Note that an *s* is added.

➤ The Latin root *fer* means "to carry." Write each of these words next to its definition.

confer   prefer   infer   refer   defer   transfer

1. _____ to carry a thing ahead of other things in your mind because you like it better

2. _____ to consult (together) with people

3. _____ to carry something from one place across to another

4. _____ to send someone for information or help

5. _____ to carry away or put off until later

6. _____ to carry your own meaning into what another person says

➤ The Latin root *tract* means "to drag," "to draw," or "to pull." Fill in the blanks with the following words to complete the sentences. The underlined words are your clues.

subtract   extract   retract   detract

contract   distract   abstract

7. Should you be forced to <u>draw back</u> a statement you made, you would

_____it.

8. When muscles are tightened, they are <u>drawn together</u> or _____ed.

9. Things that <u>pull</u> you <u>away from</u> what you are doing _____ you.

10. When we place a number <u>under</u> another number to <u>draw</u> out the difference between

them, we are _____ing.

11. If a dentist <u>pulls out</u> a tooth, she _____s it.

12. An _____idea is <u>apart from</u> a concrete object or a real thing.

13. An inapropriate frame can <u>pull</u> you <u>away from</u> the beauty of a painting; it

_____s from the picture's lovely quality.

➡ The Latin root *ject* means "to throw." Fill in the blanks with the following words to complete the sentences. The underlined words are your clues.

deject   project   object   subject

interject   reject   inject

1. The speaker threw her voice forward until it _____ed to the back of the room.

2. When we throw out our arguments against someone's plan, we are
   _____ ing to it.

3. A player who is downcast after losing a game often feels _____ ed.

4. When a nurse throws a vaccine into your arm, she is _____ing it.

5. When we toss our thoughts in between other people's comments, we
   _____ our ideas.

6. The people who were thrown under the rule of a new king became his
   _____.

7. A writer who sends stories off to be published may have her work thrown back at her if
   the stories are _____ed.

★ *tend* ("to stretch") and *mit* ("to send") are Latin roots in some common words. It will help your spelling if you recognize these roots within words. However, these roots don't always help you with word meanings.

➡ Write each of these words next to its definition.

admit   submit   transmit   permit

pretend   attend   extend   intend

8. _____to allow a person to do something

9. _____to give someone the right to enter

10. _____to yield to the power or control of another

11. _____to send over or to pass on

12. _____to stretch out

13. _____to plan; to have in mind as a purpose

14. _____to be present at

15. _____to make believe

➡ Fill in each blank with one of the words listed below.

mismatched	adjoining	convene	addict	transport
disabled	obscure	among	absorb	intersect
discovered	convict	ashore	misgivings	

1. The man was severley injured in a car wreck. Since then he has been

   _____.

2. The socks don't match. One is dark blue and the other is dark black. They are

   _____.

3. There is a traffic light where the two streets cut across each other. There is a lot of

   traffic where those streets _____.

4. The group will come together for a meeting. We will _____ before lunch.

5. A drug _____ is a person who depends on drugs and is very attached to
   them.

6. Margaret spilled water on the table. She needed something to soak it up. She found a

   sponge to _____ the water.

7. How will I carry my belongings across town? I will have to rent a truck to

   _____ them.

8. The meaning of the poem was _____.

9. Mom likes to mingle with the crowd at a party. She has fun when she's

   _____ friends.

10. You can get to Ray's room by going through Gerald's room. They have

    _____ rooms.

11. The judge had _____ about an early release from prison for the

    _____.

12. The swimmers _____ a beautiful piece of driftwood that had washed

    _____.

➡ Read the following sentences and circle all the List 14 words that you can find.

1. It was hard to translate the letter because there were so many misspellings and mistakes.

2. Martha discovered that her grandfather needed a heart transplant.

3. We hired a mover to transport the goods across town.

4. If there is interest, our team can obtain a permit and enter the contest.

5. Will you set aside your work and help me adjust the safety belts?

6. If no one objects, the teacher will dismiss the class ahead of time.

7. Albert could not contain his anger and lost control of his temper.

8. We lay awake discussing the distant land before we fell asleep.

9. It was a mistake to conduct the meeting when Jason was absent.

10. The children get into mischief and often disagree when they interact.

11. I get confused when you interrupt me.

➡ Take out a piece of blank paper. Your teacher will dictate three of the sentences above for you to write.

➡ Now select ten words from List 14 and create a short story or a descriptive paragraph that uses those words. Be creative and avoid repetition!

Reading Accuracy: Demonstrate your accuracy in reading and spelling List 14 words. Your teacher will select ten words to read and ten practical spelling words for you to spell. Record your scores on the Accuracy Checklist. Work toward 90–100 percent accuracy.

Reading Proficiency: Now build up your reading fluency with List 14 words. Decide on your rate goal with your teacher. Record your progress on the Proficiency Graph.

My goal for reading List 14 is _____ words per minute with two or fewer errors.

* awhile	* hired	* reward	* worried	interfere
* biggest	* hopefully	* scared	abstain	interject
* blankets	* invent	* shorten	abstract	mislead
* brightest	* kicked	* sloppy	adapt	misplace
* cried	* ordered	* soreness	addict	mopping
* dancing	* painted	* spilled	ashore	obscure
* describe	* peaches	* stamped	bitten	perform
* dried	* persons	* stories	consult	perturb
* easier	* placing	* studying	convict	prescribe
* foolish	* pointless	* styled	decrease	profile
* frozen	* ponies	* swinging	discard	scraper
* glasses	* priceless	* tasted	discount	striped
* grateful	* quietly	* trimmed	explode	submerge
* greater	* really	* unfinished	filed	submit
* happened	* refuse	* used	griping	transfer
* helping	* rented	* wealthy	insist	transplant

*Practical spelling words. The teacher and student should decide together how many of these words the student will be responsible for spelling.

SUMMARY OF PREFIXES

Prefix	Origin	Meaning	Key Word
re-	Latin	back, again	return
de-	Latin	down, away from	depress
sub-	Latin	below, under	subway
pro-	Latin	forward	propel
pre-	Latin	before	preschool
per-	Latin	through, completely	perspire
un-	Anglo-Saxon	not	unkind
in-	Latin	in, not	intake, insane
ex-	Latin	out	exit
a-	Anglo-Saxon	on, in	aboard
dis-	Latin	apart, opposite of	dislike
trans-	Latin	across	transmit
mis-	Anglo-Saxon	wrong, bad	misplace
con-	Latin	together, with	connect
ab-	Latin	away from	absent
ad-	Latin	to, toward	advance
ob-	Latin	against, in the way	object
inter-	Latin	between, among	interstate

SUMMARY OF ROOTS

Root	Origin	Meaning	Key Word
pel	Latin	to drive	propel
tend	Latin	to stretch	extend
spire	Latin	to breathe	inspire
form	Latin	to form	reform
spect	Latin	to see, to look	inspect
fect	Latin	to make, to do	perfect
scribe	Latin	to write	subscribe
port	Latin	to carry	export
duct	Latin	to lead	conduct
tain	Latin	to hold	contain
fer	Latin	to carry	transfer
tract	Latin	to drag, draw, pull	distract
ject	Latin	to throw	reject
mit	Latin	to send	transmit
sist	Latin	to stand	insist

Student _____

Record accuracy score as a fraction: $\dfrac{\text{\# correct}}{\text{\# attempted}}$

List	Examples	Check Test Scores Date:		Reading				Spelling			
		Reading	Spelling								
9. Consonant Suffixes and Plurals *-ly, -ty, -ful, -fully, -ment, -less, -ness, -some, -s, -es*	careless statement branches										
10. Vowel Suffixes and Spelling Rules *-ing, -er, -est, -en, -ish, -y*	biggest stranger planting										
11. Three sounds of *-ed* /d/, /t/, /əd/	tacked mailed painted										
12. Spelling Patterns – Vowel Suffixes	diner dinner										
13. Common Prefixes *re-, de-, sub-, pro-, pre-, per-, un-, in-, ex-*	inside prevent										
14. Additional Common Prefixes *a-, dis-, mis-, trans-, con-, inter-, ab-, ad-, ob-*	abstain misplace										
Review: Lists 9–14											

Student _____

Goal _____

●————● Words Read Correctly

✕————✕ Errors

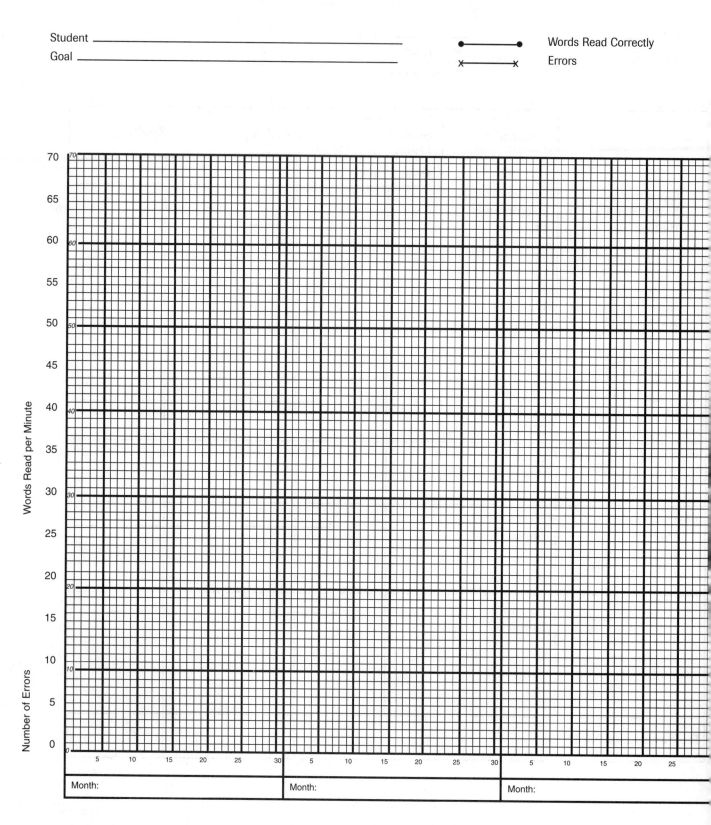

Words Read per Minute

Number of Errors

Month:

Month:

Month:

Calendar Days

PROFICIENCY GRAPH

Student _____   •——• Words Read Correctly

Goal _____   ✗——✗ Errors

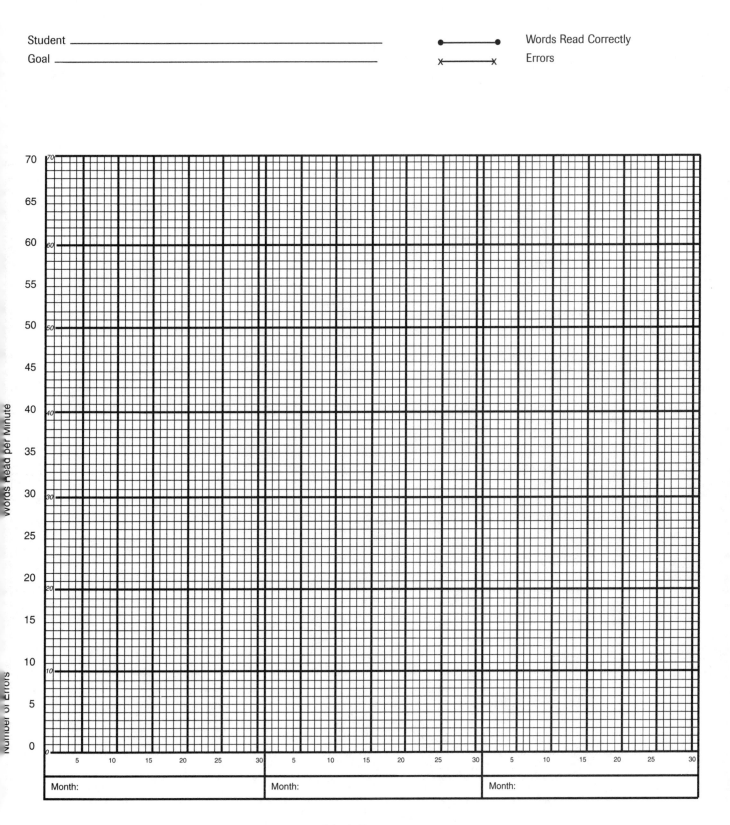

Calendar Days

PROFICIENCY GRAPH

Student _____

Goal _____

•————• Words Read Correctly

x————x Errors

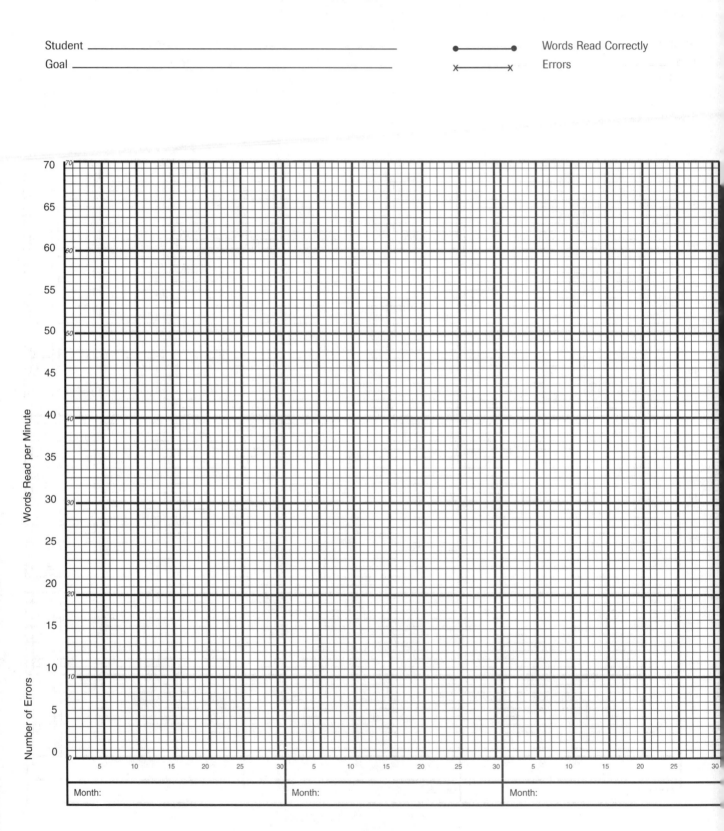

Words Read per Minute

Number of Errors

Month:

Month:

Month:

Calendar Days

EXAMINER'S RECORDING FORM – READING

Check Test: Lists 9–14

Megawords 2

Name _____

Date _____

9. Consonant Suffixes and Plurals

completely
faithfully
butterflies
government
speechless

correct _____

10. Vowel Suffixes

youngest
bringing
earlier
frighten
stylish

correct _____

11. Three sounds of *–ed*

ordered
supposed
crowded
licked
envied

correct _____

12. Spelling Patterns – Vowel Suffixes

cuter
griping
slopped
planning
filed

correct _____

13. Common Prefixes

prescribe
unfinished
submerge
protrude
persuade

correct _____

14. Additional Common Prefixes

abduct
disabled
transcend
conspire
aboard

correct _____

Total Correct _____
Total Possible ___30___

Name _____   Date _____

9. Consonant Suffixes and Plurals

completely

faithfully

butterflies

government

speechless

correct _____

10. Vowel Suffixes

youngest

bringing

earlier

frighten

stylish

correct _____

11. Three sounds of –ed

ordered

supposed

crowded

licked

envied

correct _____

12. Spelling Patterns – Vowel Suffixes

cuter

griping

slopped

planning

filed

correct _____

13. Common Prefixes

prescribe

unfinished

submerge

protrude

persuade

correct _____

14. Additional Common Prefixes

abduct

disabled

transcend

conspire

aboard

correct _____

Total Correct _____

Total Possible __30__